Chasing Apollo

Poems of Rome

By
Leah Bailey

First Printed in United Kingdom 2021

Published by Conscious Dreams Publishing
www.consciousdreamspublishing.com

Edited by Elise Abram

Typeset by Oksana Kosovan

ISBN: 978-1-913674-69-4

Dedication

For my Aunt Mae, who painted pictures
of travel with her words.
Hopefully my words will paint pictures
she'd be proud of, now, and always.

Contents

Verse 1 – Sunrise from the plane

Chasing Apollo

1.
Chasing Apollo
early morning sky,
catching up dawn.
Chasing dreams of years ago,
strange reflection on a lake.

2.
Through doubled glass
Earth's wrinkled face, bleached white,
channels run stark.
Worship-filled faces stare,
locked, awaiting time's passage.

3.
Waiting driver,
glad of transition,
no stress.
Church, palace, all beyond,
all gated or walled.

4.
Reputation,
of Italian drivers
well earned.
Lanes, patterns, nebulous
at best, afterthought signals.

5.
Mythical lift of
double doors, metal lace,
shake as it rises.
Delighted laugh as I think,
'I'm in an old film!'

6.
Check in, pay up,
a map given. Out with
determined panic.
Glad for wheeled luggage,
short walk.

7.
Another lift.
More modern, grey, small
built, negative space.
To the 5th floor
and the 3rd door, I have keys.

8.
Settle in, unpack…
more space than expected.
View from rear window,
St Peter's Dome, sunlit.
Half a day yet to explore.

9.
Change clothes
from storm to sunshine.
Blue skies, too bright glare.
Trying not to squint
as I take first view.

10.
St Peter's road,
can't get too close…
tempting to enter.
But that is planned
for the last day.

11.
Two empires
visually jarring.
Golden arches with
forced perspective, the size
of the Vatican dome.

12.
Castel S'Angelo
imposing stone forbids.
Guardian long
of Popes, of Kings,
of many things.

13.
Di Giustizia
where justice reigns,
glory in stone.
All courts should look so,
right must be powerful.

14.
Along the river
cannot get lost.
A villa in view.
When I retire, I too
want a roof garden citrus.

15.
Not far I'm caught…
colour of rusted blood,
black dead vines.
Sign says it's a school,
If anywhere looked haunted…

Verse 14 – House on the Tiber, citrus trees on the roof garden

16.
P. del Popolo
Wide open, classic.
Otherness expected,
though not adverts on canvas…
renovations paid by cars.

17.
Early to bed
tired from travel, unlike
neighbouring café.
Frightening, strange city,
unwilling to night explore.

18.
Late to rise,
make a plan, use a map,
don't get lost.
Use straight shopping road,
no interest in purchasing.

19.
First distraction,
Murano glass shop.
An earring lost
in New Year's celebration
replaced, and more…

20.
I mistake one church
for another, a second…
Santa Maria,
then Sacred Art Museum,
guises of church confuses.

21.
Cancelleria
courtyard with inventions,
Da Vinci display.
It's only been one day,
glut of sights… I must miss out.

22.
Campo di Fiore,
friend recommend for lunch…
seduction riot!
"You try some lunch?"
"Champagne in the sun, *bella*?"

23.
"Some spices!"
"Six for €10, Limoncelle?"
"We have for you…"
"Lunch, lovely lady…?"
From all sides calls come.

24.
I must look English,
no attempt at others,
but something draws.
I return to the first,
as I promised I would.

25.
Treated a queen,
in sun enthroned,
champagne to await
coffee and pizza…
effortless persuasion.

26.
Word after word…
watch him work magic.
Five tongues I *know*…
seamless switches to suit
charisma beyond station.

27.
Little old man,
with a denim bag,
offers me poems.
English and Italian,
dedicated, "to mother".

28.
He signs it,
I discover
I can still be moved
to tears… by verse.
I thought that long lost.

29.
Pizza arrives,
four cheese, thin crust,
dripping taste and oil.
Sun shines, server smooths,
a still world, in a crowd.

30.
Part of me
longs to stay lost
here in the sun.
Follow the plan, yet…
"You come back, go out tonight."

Verse 33 – Largo di Torre Argentina

31.
Silken offer,
how smooth is *too* smooth?
The night does call me.
Assured he's a gentleman,
I consider returning.

32.
Had planned to retrace
to Piazza Navona.
Afraid I'd get lost,
turn for The Pantheon,
stumble across the unplanned.

33.
Among traffic,
millennia old,
lost in time... Largo
di Torre Argentina.
Unbearable beauty.

34.
Temples from BC,
long after the gods are gone,
church that replaced them,
also gone, alter remains,
among remains of stone.

35.
Tiny town square,
found accidentally,
in a town flooded
with such remains...
should stop surprising me.

36.
Two streets away
The Pantheon awaits.
Before that though,
a curious ruin, with
no label, built around.

37.
What was it for?
Why build around it?
Why no label?
The mystery allows
so many choices to mind.

38.
Two thousand years,
almost, worshipping
god or gods remains
strong within. Solid walls,
huge pillars guard the door.

39.
Inside, such space,
feeling of solidity
has not faded.
Awed, wishing sight through time,
see ancient ways through modern.

40.
Weight above, felt
yet not, hold my breath, silence.
Some tourists.
Others need reminders
this is still a church.

Verse 38 – The Pantheon, front view

41.
Oculus beams
sun, sweeping like Apollo,
above the bones
of Raphael's rest.
Among Gods old and new.

42.
A courtyard beckons,
palm trees, sunshine, confusion.
Entrance? No entrance?
No… around corners, up stairs.
Ticket, no guides in English.

43.
Ceilings and walls,
mosaic floors,
flat columns painted.
Carved and gilded…
no art but the room itself.

44.
Shading and light
make the flat seem textured,
tricks the eye.
Rooms of state, from states
long past, echoes.

45.
Something haunting
in staircases of stone.
Above or below.
What's there tempts the mind,
light plays in spirals.

46.
Finally entered,
museum fare offered;
disturbing statue
of a child's victory.
Child as scary as demon.

47.
Ceiling frescos
as evocative as
any display.
Complex scenes, mosaic
masters managers marry.

48.
Moulded flowers
on ceramic vases,
moulded heroes
on the king of steins.
Skill, frivolity, as one.

49.
Diana, goddess,
wisdom and curves… how I wish
veneration came.
A time when hips and curves
were worshipped, not sent to gyms.

50.
The Figura
Allegorica
Femminile.
A title I feel
in every part of my flesh.

51.
I envy Venus
depiction of rounded form.
Realistic desire.
When did we lose wanting
real goddesses, soft, rounded?

52.
Courtyard air
brings pause to diversion.
Displays dazzle
and the stair again captures
my imagination.

53.
From Palazzo
of Venetzia past,
to Victory.
Façade of monuments
not as old as they appear.

54.
Architecture
belies its young age,
view incomparable.
City in the round,
appropriately labelled.

55.
Feels ancient,
inside honours the soldiers,
Victory's worshipers.
Mounted charioteers,
like Gods, forever marching.

56.
Seen from the top,
imagine Trajan's market
bursting with life.
Almost 2,000 years old,
I long to shop its wares.

57.
Last sight I planned,
steps to Capitolina.
Do I go back now?
Night out with a local
seems the best way to start.

58.
Navigating
by river, can't get lost.
I decide to go.
Dressed for a night out,
I return to the café.

59.
Restaurant rock star,
my guide seems... everywhere.
No reservation,
at a table in the back,
Achille Al Pantheon.

60.
Smooth as silk,
Wine, food (that's on no menu)
arrives in a rush.
Walk through ruins, all lit up,
post-dinner drinks smoother still.

Verse 56 – Trajan's Market, view from the Victory Monument

61.
Well-spent evening,
more comfortable now,
going out at night.
Though a gentleman, for sure,
I choose to keep it light.

62.
However nice,
no complications wanted
for days or nights.
A dinner or two with
company is enough.

63.
Today's adventure,
in brightest sunshine,
Scalinata di
Trinit à dei Monti.
Map kindly tells what's what.

64.
The column of
immaculate conception,
irony in stone.
A boat displaced in flood,
Bernini made a fountain.

65.
An English surprise...
Keat's house in renovation,
open shop only.
English poet, his last days
spent where my poem is set.

Verse 66 – Spanish steps

66.
Climb in the sun
among all the tourists,
the others, that is.
Sometimes it's good
to follow the crowd.

67.
Built by many hands
on site of Aqua Virgo,
beautiful fountain.
Buzzing with people, sunshine;
sculpted water paradise.

68.
Gelato nearby,
heavenly flavours,
perfect, peaceful, calm.
Wedding photos amid crowds,
many coins in the fountain.

69.
Seeking things between
fountain and Coloso,
lost, but not lost.
Palace for exhibitions
tempts me to turn from my plans.

70.
I resist this one,
but not the next, a church.
Smaller St Peter's,
surprising with beauty
to house chains for a saint.

Verse 70 – Basilica of San Pietro in Vincoli, found while lost

71.
Think I find the way,
Via delle Sette Sale,
but there's no out.
I finally find the park
'midst Nero's ruins they play.

72.
From the green I stare
at a Coloso, apt name.
Built for people,
to replace a madman's lake.
I look forward to a tour.

73.
Arch of Constantine
spans Via Triumphalis,
Emperor's entrance.
Reliefs ironically stolen,
Trajan, Hadrian and more.

74.
Consistent Caesar,
riding beneath the thieves
that came before.
Now his statue stands
on debated murder site.

75.
Sunset behind me,
sillouetting the ruin...
near two thousand years.
A glorious end to a
glorious wandering day.

Verse 74 – Statue of Julius Caesar, debated place murdered

Verse 75 – Colosseum at sunset, from outside

76.
Capuchin Crypt,
mortality reminder.
Remains displayed
of hundreds of monks,
taking turns in holy soil.

77.
Early morning
to think about the end,
macabre display
to sacrifice the dead
to edify the living.

78.
Villa Borghese,
main goal for today,
map is deceiving.
Lost again, wandering Rome.
Who knows what I'll find?

79.
Gladiators!
I fall in a tourist trap.
Photos on the path,
price given only *after*;
I should have avoided.

80.
Above the path,
Piazza del Popolo
In panorama.
Near Villa de Medici
all Rome seems at my feet.

Verse 82 – In the park of Borghese Villa, headless muse

81.
Still lost,
but on a closer hilltop
to Borghese.
Finally the gate appears,
may still make my entrance time.

82.
Lush, green, rolling hills,
dappled sunshine, benches
and statues preside.
Headless muse, ironically,
holds the head of comedy.

83.
After the fear
of missing my entrance time,
a wait in the sun.
Going to the shop first
feels wrong, but I have the time.

84.
V. Suburbana,
Scipione Borghese's,
to house collections.
Eclectic museum,
no purpose but display.

85.
Nephew of the Pope,
patron of Bernini,
indulged in art.
Never made as a home,
housing masters' works of art.

86.
A Cardinal shows
wealth, power, prestige of worth;
rooms named by contents.
First of its kind, unique,
still an unmissable sight.

87.
No pictures within,
only memories, a flood,
ev'ry inch calls me.
Floor to ceiling beauty,
I'm breathless with awe.

88.
Statues stare,
frescoes hover like heaven
only the entrance.
I'm David to Goliath,
but I'm the one struck down.

89.
Scandalous marble,
19th century princess,
Venus Victrix.
Reclining wife and sister,
nobility *too* unclothed.

90.
Room of the Sun,
Apollo's quadratura,
painted on ceilings.
Antique sculpture fragments
surround Bernini's David.

91.
The nymph, Daphne,
forever runs from Apollo,
forever captured.
Centuries of pursuit
beneath scenes of Ovid's tale.

92.
Room of Emperors,
replica sculptures and bust,
'neath Galatea.
Jealousy of Gods seems fit
for candelabra grotesques.

93.
Central Bernini
of poor Proserpina,
Pluto possessed.
A gallery fit to glory
the dominance of gods.

94.
Undoubted beauty
in the replicated form,
Hermaphrodite.
Illusionist frames show out
on lush fields of the ancient.

95.
Disappointing lack
of gladiators in
Gladiator room.
Gods arguing over Troy
above Aeneas statue.

96.
The rooms begin
to overwhelm the senses,
Egypt, Silenus...
don't want to miss a single
Caravaggio, new floor.

97.
Galleries still huge,
first floor is rich with colour.
Smaller side rooms.
I feel able to focus,
not overwhelmed by statues.

98.
The last three rooms
named for statues sold to Louvre,
but ceilings astound.
Artist names spin my head,
don't know art, but I know them.

99.
Raphael, Sarto,
Botticelli, Cosimo...
jaw-dropping beauty.
Paintings so classic
I could lose myself in them.

100.
Lanfranco fresco,
open Loggia now closed,
Council of the Gods.
Views of the garden, divine...
what lavish gatherings were?

101.
Before the passage,
Bassano's 'Last Supper',
I get wondering
how many times has
this been the subject of art?

102.
Lost, once again,
in masters on ceilings,
room on room passes.
So sorrowful I couldn't
take more than mental pictures.

103.
Overwhelmed
from the riot of colour,
green sculpted patterns
behind are a relief.
Disintegrating statues.

104.
Contrast the inside
with its protected pieces,
exposed, crumbling Gods.
Next to the open, walled,
secret pathways of citrus.

105.
Follies and facades
bookend alcoves and iron,
lace-like, fences, gates...
Exclusion makes you wonder,
imagine, parties within.

Verse 105 – Private gardens of Villa Borghese

106.
Planned evening
brings me back to the Trevi.
Sunset colour paints,
while I pass time with wine
in apt named Trattoria.

107.
Wine at Lacanda
Giulietta e Romeo
kind to let me wait.
Dinner tonight with my guide.
Might come back here to eat.

108.
Sunset o'er Trevi,
my guide takes pictures of me,
coins in the fountain.
A lovely, simple dinner
disdained by my snobby guide.

109.
He's spent too long
as a hospitality
rock star in Rome
to be satisfied with
something so close to tourists.

110.
A late night drinking,
means a late morning starting,
and it softly rains.
Today must be a light one,
for tomorrow will be hard.

111.
Last, full, unclaimed day,
time to indulge the shopping.
Finding what I thought
I wanted, not so easy,
not even sure what I want.

112.
Gladiator's blade
tempts me on the road
in St. Peter's view.
Beautiful replica etched,
silver, heavy in my hand.

113.
As a Protestant
what saints are for what?
Hope the shops can help.
A family of teachers
needs all the help it can get.

114.
Delighted to find
Patron saint of Teachers
is a woman.
St Catherine from Egypt,
Alexandria visions.

115.
But no metals found,
antique coins no longer sold,
all my ideas nought.
Perhaps I'll stumble later
on what seems right for gifts.

116.
Bag is heavy
with drink and spices,
I can't resist.
But now I head to church,
Basilica St. Clement.

117.
Just one sight today,
much more than I bargained for
lay within its walls.
Descending the stairs is like
descending the centuries.

118.
Nineteenth-century priest,
finds the fourth-century church
beneath his own.
Beneath that even older...
first and second century past.

119.
Former Mithraeum,
Mithraic altar and school,
original river.
Possibly Vespasian's
mint for the empire of Rome.

120.
Not just it's past,
but preserved in the present,
Triumphal arch with
Apse mosaic... awe stirring,
breath holding, wonder of art.

Verse 121/2 – Gladiator Barracks near Colosseum

121.
Outside, more to come,
unexpected barracks wait,
a preserved *ludas*.
In the shadow of their death,
fighters waited near to hell.

122.
Grass has now grown in
on what's left of the cells where
survival was life.
Between this day and sunset
Colosso remnants still rule.

123.
Best of the last now,
Citta del Vaticano,
early morning tour.
Mother of Caligula
built gardens near his circus.

124.
Through the secure gates
guide glides us to the courtyard,
shaded and chilly.
Details of art in advance
as Sistine silence is known.

125.
Museum bound we
blink in the sun's first rays.
Crowds chase guides
to the best open spaces
for each explanation.

126.
Sculpture of ages,
both modern and ancient,
some seem out of place.
Fragments line the walls, a glut
of incomplete and unmarked.

127.
No hall unadorned,
even entrances engraved,
artistry excess.
Everywhere I look, my eyes
feed on the exotic sights.

128.
Cold courtyard coffins,
like the dead Gods that surround
conquered trophies here.
Octagonal space presents
masterpieces popes collect.

129.
Carvings of stone,
so white they seem of ivory,
crowds move among them.
Hadrian's garden Hermes
beside River God Arno.

130.
Perseus holds high
detached head of Medusa,
flanked by warriors.
Laocoon and sons forever
bound to battle as we watch.

Verse 131 – Muse of poetry in the Vatican Museum

131.
Museum proper,
where even statue storage
is a feast for eyes.
Round Apollo's broken bust
his muses all displayed.

132.
Pantheon mimic,
domed roof to mosaic floor.
Imperial bath
of porphyry, looked on by
stone sentries, emperors past.

133.
Moments of glory,
marbled memory surrounds us.
Each adds their visage...
originally meant to
deify, now mere statues.

134.
Fine figures of men,
golden rays light Hercules,
bold, bronzed... bestial.
Ancient acquisition,
displayed as conquered hero.

135
First 'photoshop' try,
Emperor Claudius' head
on model's body.
Vanity in one's image...
not a modern invention.

Verse 132 – Room with statues of Caesars, Hercules VM

136.
Honoured Constantine,
honours his sainted mother
and his daughter.
Purple marble, porphyry,
entombs in Etruscan room.

137.
A room just to show
The Biga… first century
restored chariot.
Is preservation for pride,
or responsibility?

138.
Galleries ensue:
candelabra, tapestries,
maps of the known world.
Angels of virtue above,
Life of Jesu on the wall.

139.
Though the maps astound,
it's the ceiling I stare at
in marvelled silence.
Last of the museum,
next is Sistine silence.

140.
No pictures, no words.
None allowed, none sufficient…
to come even *close*.
Fifteen minutes only,
to *try* to fix it in mind.

141.
I went in a year
when Raphael's birthday
was being honoured.
Five hundred years old,
they hung his tapestries there.

142.
So, all in one room...
Raphael, Botticelli,
Perugino...
Roselli, Lecce, Broeck...
Others... Michelangelo...

143.
I get as annoyed
as the guards at the tourists
who ignore the rules.
How do you stand in that room
and not hold your breath, your speech?

144.
Regardless of your
faith, or lack of, just the *art*,
needs your reverence.
The stories told by my guide
come echoing back.

145.
Panel by panel,
completed near on his own,
Riots of colour.
The *Last Judgement* of God was
also Michelangelo's.

Verse 148/9 – St. Peter's Basilica and square

146.
Critics saw themselves,
captured in the frescos',
eternal judgement.
The artist placed himself there,
a self-portrait of flayed skin.

147.
The sculptor's pain,
forced to paint instead of sculpt,
for many years.
I'm in awe of his skill,
his resilience, always.

148.
Reunited group
moves to the courtyard out front,
St Peter's main door.
On St Peter's square, vastness,
above me, around me.

149.
The sheer weight of time,
beliefs focused in one spot,
hopes laid at the door.
Many doors, including one
that opens once a decade.

150.
I imagine it,
a doorway that forgives all...
ev'ry broken rule.
I can't decide if I would
even want to be forgiv'n.

Verse 151 – The nave of St. Peter's Basilica, overwhelming

151.
Beyond the door...
undimmed, unchanged opulence.
Awe-inspiring
monument in marble,
gilding and statuary.

152.
Like the museum,
Faith-filled or not...
the breath catches,
the heart stops and races,
ev'ry sight weighted with time.

153.
The hist'ry past here,
started here, ended here:
Kings, Queens, Popes and more.
Soldiers and commoners,
traders and tourists all come.

154.
Walk the marble floor
above St Peter's bones...
below arches, domes...
among tombs, statues, organs...
momentarily as one.

155.
Hours not enough,
will return to see it all...
beauty and wonder.
Sunlight streams on frescos
and statues still in my dreams.

Verse 154 – Organ in a side isle

Verse 155 – Michelangelo statue in St Peter's

156.
A brief lunch follows,
May heat in February,
ev'n surprises guides.
The Colosseum is next,
numbered arches gape welcome.

157.
Centuries ago
people entered for free...
each to their own door.
Built on Nero's drained lake,
politics, propaganda.

158.
Prisoners of war,
conquered Gauls and Thracians,
Lanista bought slaves,
even freedmen, for profit,
or glory, bleed in same sand.

159.
Guide tells stories,
guidebook tells even more...
of this colosso.
Building whose varied life
did not end with the empire.

160.
Glaring sunlight bakes
the view I try to capture,
unsuccessfully.
Like this ruin's hist'ry,
can't confine this colossus.

Verse 160 – Inside the Colosseum, bright sunshine

161.
View from the exit,
Piazza De Colosso,
Temple of Venus,
and the Arch of Constantine.
Walking under the first time.

162.
I begin to think,
doing both tours in one day
was a big mistake.
I see the steps I must climb
to the hill of Romulus.

163.
Empire begun
in legend and in fact.
Ancients' seat...
Aneas met; Romulus,
Remus left in Lupercal.

164.
Occupied for near
three-thousand years,
the remains astound.
Domus Tiberiana,
altered by emperors.

165.
What remains,
ruinous though it is,
implies splendour.
Imaginary frescos,
gardens, fountains, marbles... more.

Verse 166 – Stadio of the Emperor on Palatine Hill

166.
Stadio arcade
with emperor's seat midway,
private palace path.
Domus Augustana, where
marble floor can still be walked.

167.
Lower courtyard
fountain remains elegant;
what a house it was.
How overwhelming
to commoners called.

168.
Stand on the white stone
marking the place of the throne;
touch where wealth dined...
served by slaves, on cushions,
heated floors, delicacies.

169.
Renaissance gardens,
pavilions, exotic plants...
Famese family
view of the Roman forum
makes Domus Rome's best address.

170.
Wind down forum's hill
to walk the Via Sacra,
Processions' road.
Pain is intense, so tired,
six hours of touring.

Verse 168 – Dining room floor where the Emperors dined

Verse 169 – The View of the Roman forum from D. Tiberiana

171.
Road I walk, mended,
repeatedly paved,
in Caesar's footsteps.
Through arches, past black marble,
where Romulus was killed.

172.
Circular bricks show
Umbilicus Urbis,
centre of Rome,
contact point, world of the dead.
On this ground it echoes.

173.
Saturn's Temple,
house of father to Gods
and state treasure.
Augustus marked it with
where empire roads converge.

174.
Julius Temple,
where Caesar was deified
and cremated,
is preserved on central square.
The weight of this space confounds.

175.
Gemini remains
in temple to the twins,
three columns still stand.
Temple of Vesta, flame
eternal gone out, still stands.

Verse 171 – Via Sacra in the Roman Forum, worn by many

Verse 178 – Nighttime walk past Castel Saint Angelo

176.
Tour finally ends,
try to absorb all I've seen…
impossible task.
I rest and get ready
for my last dinner in Rome.

177.
La Zanzara…
let the waiter choose the wine,
indulge my palate.
My guide joins me this last meal,
company improves good food.

178.
A beautiful close
to my last day in Rome…
sweet farewells,
smiles and laughter
with a good friend.

179.
The morning to pack,
leave cases by the door,
a few hours left.
Last wander in the sun,
Isola Tiberina.

180.
On the first day,
crossed here before turning in,
street artists sell here.
I hope to find the same one,
buy more of his works.

Verse 179 – Isola Tiberiana, last day in the sunshine...

181.
Basilica song
draws me over the bridge,
await service end.
San Bartolomeo...
Baroque martyrs' memorial.

182.
Unexpected gem,
artifacts of martyrs...
some known, some unknown.
Reminded how good it is
to get lost in Rome, and found.

183.
Modern hospital
where ancient healing temple
once served apart.
Porticoes for the temple
to Aesculapius.

184.
Across from café
is the artist I seek,
difficult choices.
Too many watercolours,
very little time.

185.
Once chosen,
the haggling begins,
a fair price is found.
Happy with my last purchase,
wander slowly back in sun.

186.
Transport arrives,
driving back the way I came,
looks different now.
Now I know this city,
part of my heart will remain.

187.
As I fly away,
touching setting Apollo's
realm above the clouds...
the colours dim but will ne'er
be forgotten; I'll return.

Verse 187 – Sunset as I fly away...

Riding Into Dawn

Dim and growing light, the sun rises slow...
like waking from a dream both dark and full,
shades of colour shift, brighten until we know
the banking of the plane, soft enough, a lull.
The morning's glowing in roses and gold,
shifting glamour as if fairy magic, lurid light
from slumbered stupor is breaking its hold,
banishing the world from the spell of night.
Our eyes are drawn by Apollo's power
to dawning's charm and the start of day,
speculating, musing what could this hour
of the new possible bring stumbling our way.
Fixed, enchanted, the moment's still
in trance of rapture for spectre of sun
enthralled, immobile, captured our will,
fascination between moments, till done.

Within Walls

Why all the walls
Around all that I see?
Keep out or keep in?

Parks and palaces,
Houses hold their secrets.
Curiosity.

Rome's secrets beckon
From within, behind walls.
Open the gates.

Overload of the Eternal

It was called the eternal city, I always knew,
but I didn't know how much this was true.
There's a map that's marked, all the sights,
but the map and my senses seem to fight.
It can't possibly show it all, since everywhere
it seems fascinating surroundings stare.
Eternal because there isn't enough time,
you'd need eternity to be able to find,
explore, each building you'd enjoy seeing,
accepting being overwhelmed is freeing.
Knowing no matter how much I might want
to see everything, choose not to let it haunt.
Deciding instead I will have to come back,
using photos and notes to keep track
of what I've already seen, in this visit.
A plan to repeatedly return isn't bad, is it?
Building layer upon layer of memory treasure,
like the city built itself, it will live forever.

Plans Within Plans

Spiraling out from the hotel, I must make a plan.
After yesterday's learning, that the eternal will
overwhelm...
I know I *must* make a plan, or face the possibility
that I won't see anything, for fear of not seeing
everything...

How do I decide what to do? How do I choose?
Do I use a map with a preplanned route,
defined?
How far can I walk, in a single day, on foot?
Dare I go on foot, with the risk of being
distracted?

The planned routes, last until the first
side street's siren call pulls me toward
unknown...
Unplanned, unknown joys and delights
pull me off the path, but I always try to
return...

I guess at how far I can go and not tire,
my feet tell me more about the distance
travelled....
I keep track of how far I've gone, to be
proud of myself, for burning off weights of
pasta...

I wonder what tomorrow's plan should be...
I wonder if I'll stick to it, or let myself get
lost...
Maybe I'll do a day without plan, just to
See what happens without one to be my
guide...

Spirit of Nero

More time spent before, not after, being an emperor.
14 years of rule, begun at 17 years of age.
A madness of rule, mother aided at the start,
Married to an emperor's daughter, favoured above
An emperor's son, who died after being passed.

Mother murderer, for plotting to kill him.
Wife murderer, accused of barrenness, adultery...
Father of a dead daughter, second wife murdered.

Fiddled while Rome burned, so they say...
Taking advantage of cleared ground,
His 'golden' palace to build, taxing to supply...
Taxing people already displeased, suspicious.

Britain rebels, other fights lost, he is weakened,
Province of Gaul supports Spain over him.
Senate declares him an enemy of the people.
Guards who made him, Praetorian, protectors,
Now renounce him... and Rome is lost,
All that is left is his death, by his hand.

Now, today, centuries later, the irony exists.
On a hill overlooking the icon that replaced
The lake he had for his own park, pleasure,
On a hill where his golden palace was buried
To pretend he never existed, 'enemy' of the people.

There, while lost, I found it, laughter in sun.
Among the ruins, where Nero played, fiddled,
Among the ruins, halls filled with dirt, revealed,
Among the ruins, children play, and laugh.

Sitting in the sunshine, resting from wandering,
I had been lost, looking for something, not this.
But being lost I found something unexpected...

This... among what was once decadent halls,
Among the walls where actors sang and played,
Where frescos were painted, where plots were made,
Where mothers and wives were murdered,
Where guards 'most' loyal betrayed him.
Here, here is where the innocents play.
A park green with life, alive with laughter.

Laughing louder than the children, is me.
Laughing louder than the children, is history.
Laughing louder than the children, is Nero.
The irony of attempts at destruction...
Immortalizing, preserving, echoing instead.

On the Seas of Time Travel

Time expands, and contracts,
Like breathing,
Or blinking,
Or flying.

Time fills its sails,
Like a frigate,
Or butterfly,
Or kite.

Time rolls, and ripples,
Like the Tiber,
Or champagne,
Or tears.

You can dip into it,
Like a memory,
Or dessert,
Or sauces.

You can regret leaving,
Like an unfinished task,
Or a missed date,
Or a lost earring.

You can hope to return,
Like a target,
Or strategy,
Or goal.

You can go forward,
Like imagination,
Or creation,
Or dream.

Travel in time now,
To a place
To a feeling
To a moment.

Breathe...

Verse Ending – Last rays of the sun, from the plane, as I leave

Acknowledgements

I'd like to thank my friends and family for their unwavering support and encouragement, my test readers who helped me fight my imposter syndrome and put forward more of my journeys. I'd like to thank the incredibly talented poets and artists I've met this last year as we moved open mics online and global for keeping me plugged in to the energy of inspiration from the safety of my keyboard. Especially Dee Bailey and Simply Deez Events (for getting the ball rolling), *The Life Inna Lockdown* ladies and gents, Gary Huskisson (for getting me into the open mic rooms) and *Here Comes Everyone Magazine* and Fire & Dust open mic (for being my 'first' online mic).

I'd like to thank the team at Conscious Dreams Publishing, Book Journey Mentor, Daniella Blechner; editor, Elise Abram and typesetter Oksana Kosovan for continuing to give me my voice.

About the Author

 Raised in the US but living permanently in the UK since 2003, Leah has an international point of view when it comes to the inspirational nature of the world around her. As a teacher of English Language and Literature for ten years, and as a writer of poetry and fiction for more than 25, Leah has dedicated her life to the written word and its ability to inspire and connect people. Connect them to the world around them, their own thoughts and emotions, and the experiences we all share as we travel the paths of our lives.

Leah holds degrees in English, Comparative Literature and International Studies from Pennsylvania State University in the United States as well as a Minor in German Language and Literature. At Canterbury Christ Church University, Leah trained for a PGCE in teaching secondary English, Media Studies and Drama.

Most days are spent sharing her passion for the written word with young people, trying to comprehend British slang and making sure her coffee cup is never empty for the health and safety of others. She resides in Wimbledon, assisted in looking for inspiration by her cats: Lord Merlin and Queen Mab.

Other Books by Leah Bailey

"What lies behind us, and what lies ahead of us, are tiny matters compared to what lies within us."

~ Ralph Waldo Emerson

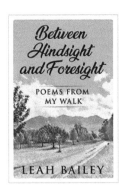

What happens when you look in the mirror when you have a day that is such a day that you can't move past it? Then there are those moments you cling to, through slippery child-like fingers, in childhood and long after, that you don't ever want to move past.

In this book of poems are snapshots and moments of one life, a walk from teenage years through to what we all laughingly call adulthood. Like memories, some are exactly as they were- word for word- the day they were put to paper 20 years ago.

Like dreams, some of them have been shaped into watercolors, through the reflection of a mirror, or tears. Come, share in the moments, rifle through the snapshots, so we can laugh and cry and enjoy them together.

Links to more about my work:

 @leahthedreamer   *Leah-The-Dreamer*

 Leah_the_dreamer   *Works of Leah-The-Dreamer*

Conscious Dreams
PUBLISHING

Be the author of your own destiny

www www.consciousdreamspublishing.com

✉ info@consciousdreamspublishing.com

Let's connect

Lightning Source UK Ltd.
Milton Keynes UK
UKHW022203090921
390242UK00008B/91